Laying flowers on the boundary

Carolyn Srygley Moore

POSTHUMAN POETRY & PROSE

**First published in the world by POSTHUMAN POETRY
& PROSE 2024**

Cover photograph **Carolyn Srygley Moore**
Cover design & editing **David C. McLean**

ISBN: 978-1-4461-7418-0

Table of Contents

Listening to Eleanor

What are you afraid of he says

The moonstone isn't made of steel
  Is it?   The red wolf yields
  The full arc rainbow
  Unlike the broken horseshoe barks
Of hounds.

Ride the wolf, Mrs x.
Round the carapace the other side of dawn.

What are you drowning in?

Can't force yourself to drown he says.
I see your mouth flounder
Your lips flutter

  Against the will of terror.
What are you afraid of? Don't dive
  Down down

& pluck the anchor.

The way to sail sail
The way to ride the wolf

  Is to pretend
  Pretend a little
  Never ever to lie — rainbow

Atlantis to the Alaskan triangle —:
Never to lie.

Rune seed

Maybe it's the stuff of ruins, history.
Rumors. Anthony & Cleopatra

Just wind chimes above a board game.
Can't recall the story

But something whispers:
Nobody was Egyptian. O fairy tales
   Woven

O fairy tales. The old woman
Cut off her own heel
To fit into the shoe. Savage was the magic.

Somebody told me
   A cloud was a human body
   A bodyguard

Between ourselves & God.
Maybe she was wrong, but the earth

Is never wrong, is it —: ripe
   As red plums
   Yellow fleshed within.

Those answers it offers
Without being asked. Those runes
   Velveteen as the rabbit

Sprung from a tear
A homesickness—. Hewn pebbles
Displacing

Faces

   Ambiguous rumors

Where ashes & urns &
   Red clay vases spill
   Seed.

Meeting Borges

Sunlight red neon in the eyes
I sat across a room from Borges.

I remember nothing
But a crowd of academics crowded
Around him; a woman asked why Borges
Chose a specific number for a specific

Motel door — he laughed, his laugh floated
A bit & never landed.

The crowds of tweed coats & A line skirts
Ushered the man out of the hall.

I liked Borges' voice, for absolutely
No reason.

It was a small car
Into which he ducked like a secret into
A girl's pocket.

I knew that the author
Had liked my laugh — I'd laughed for
Him, my earring rattling, in a small room

Full of many faces — he had
Tilted his head my way briefly.

Mirage of course, but the thought was
Agreeable & made me calm. It meant
Nothing of course. But like the burn
Of a cigarette, it kept me calm.

Self-declaration

I was naive enough to crawl
Naked into green boughs
   Painted trees acrylic layers
& curtsy once or twice that scarlet dress
An apostolic mimicry

Toward someone who will stay with me
   Forever
Amidst graffiti connoting bands
& Saturday
Morning cartoons
   Eating chips with the German
Shepherd

"

Fog bank & blank

"

O riddlers!

You who tried to take me
From my own knowledge
You who called me
To my own erasure — photographs floating
   Like scissoring mites
   Through my pores

"

I do not whimper

"

That
Nickname
Only I & I will ever witness
   A mourning dove nesting
Amidst poison & briers

A ledge of a house
Mostly on fire.

That afternoon of sand sculptures

"

Built upon remains
Architectural anthropological forensic

   You gasped as
   We built faces upon
My face & honey now
Been so long
Can't tell
   Where the first one was

(Are these other people's mirrors)

Face smooth as sky & me
Remembering

   Dusks
   Buried

Alive. Mirages layer themselves
Shutter the shut ins
With their cold roast beef & lemon meringue
Pie
   Like skin
   Healing
   Closure
   Voiding
The wound with too many names.

Running Parallel

All he can see are shorelines
Run parallel, without
Intersection
   No passage within
Possible creation. What happens to all
The drawbridges
Catching his breath
   As a ship shafts through.
Nothing is painless, or pointless
He
Hopes
   As pebbles fly
Arousing nothing
But a gull or two
Pushing a sand
   Grain
   Like a skinned boulder guitar-hollowed
Up up up
A laughing gas balloon
   Up up up.

Visiting Brooklyn

The prison across the alley
A roof straight-edge concrete anti/refuge
   Razor barbs

"

Nearby, a man who
I never loved truly —: but kissed / almost/

Amidst old jokes & jungle gyms.
Thus the memory amps

In Brooklyn.

"

   The prison across the slight alleyway is no prison

— Matisse nudes dancing blue —

& I've few regrets . Only some remorse.
I guess it must be like this

"

   Gentle Lies
That don't protect us come back,
Sometimes become
   Our flight from freedom, starlings
Crashing up cerulean blue
Shadows veer into webbed night.

A Shut In

Eleven twenty a.m.
Weekdays
  The little dog would snuffle
  & stir, scratch
  His red sofa cushion /
A man
Grey with fierce ski slope eyes
  Slate
  Blue
Peering for the next gate /
  Roused
  Mildly cracking his rocky
Bronze knuckles\
  & saw a cloud rise like
  Mercurial
Elements striking a train platform rise
  From the gravel
Path
Leading to his
Gated
  TV dinners & voluptuous orchid laced
  Garden door.

Watched the Tanks Come In

Sleepwalking midst sketching
   A dancer's motions (though it's made of brass)

   She enters the aggressive
Submissions of last tango / rent
   Zigzag Brando's eye
Struck by horizon sandy
limitations —:
   Pinched flabby jowls slit
Near tears. Tango, tango, what dance is this,
Rose thorn ripping lips
   Yet no blood, nothing
   — What is the human
Sweetness once fact once
Recognized—

   Cheers

   One loose petal
A face / place / existential collision. Red
   50's corvette wrecking an ivy
& lilac stanchion, split
Like a human being quartered
   As in a trance
 We bicycle & steamship
Backward
   The Plague
   The seaside pyres afire of the time
   Dark, too many gods,
Not enough gods.

The barn

Ransacked
  By doves & time
Stood a burnished red structure

  & midnights
The woman in paw print scrubs
Leaned
  In the farmhouse porch doorway
Her trace doubled
By her breath & smoke
  Coming from her naked mouth
Like the conversation bubbles
 Comic strips
Innocuous
  Moans groans mumbles.

The woman, 45 or so — newly
Learning
  The rippled cadence
Of her own name — was evolving
Like a tadpole inky
  Or the octopus cursive
  Drip
Drip
Through the lucent sea. Everything
Everyone
Was exciting —

& a white feral
Cat
  Swinging a piss colored plume
  Tail
Flashed

The dash
On the sarcophagi in

Nested
Like a bell
Suddenly trusting
   That space behind the blue
Broom flush yellow
In the porch corner

   Usually too near the human
Scent, the anxious, always waiting the
Knock // the call.

dusk

Moon rising blind writes me —:
Summon those damn
Minions
Make them tamed.
"

You've seen the movie. Dragons
Ridden by children
    Elephants
& ghost-dogs only.
"

Nothing
Like being told to quell the cryptoids
By someone who doesn't get it -/
        caught in headlight -/
"

They quiver &
Leap
Wisdom in tango
    Writing their selves to be mated
Angel & human..
"

        Breton's Nadja told
The spellbinding / gauze
Wrapped round & round
Cocoon or wound / gauze
"

Moon rising blind
Buckled like broken raincoat belts
The mummy the sleeping sundial
"

(Still still we /
I speak too loud we /
I bury myself alive & still
Someone hears the whistling.)

Crush

Whirling purple cotton candy
At the carnival
We had sticky hands.

We were 11.
Leah was cool. Brown hair hanging down
　　She tossed her head
Sang to the top of her voice
　　when the school bus landed.

Cotton candy on our mouths
She sang
Like a famous person
　　Not giving a damn.

She sang.

Soft spot for monsters & migrating geese

Sometimes I kiss you like death is not
  The uncanny
    prognosis

  Dashes on gravestones
  Upon which moonlight slips & rides
Like magic carpets or cloud scatter rugs

  Working night shift
 In old rundown farmhouses //
Misunderstood dogs & people
  A soft spot for

Monsters

  Floating
  Levitating
  Spirit-ash & ember tracing & tracking

That roof ledge — risk dancing — amidst
That treachery

(— A V of geese
  Southward pink neon
  Sundown like fire catch tail feathers
& suddenly I know where we are.)

Mayakovsky

He never found an umbrella
That could eclipse his view of the Milky Way
  No tarp no parasol no parachute
Oblique stitched of shadow.

Amazed.

He was
  Amazed, star-pasture
Dwarfed by nothing
Unlike most landscapes // damn corridor
Through which we are slipped
Tunneling
  Through tambourines torn,
  Promise
  Hurt, the question
As a castaway soliloquy

  "Do you want to be a pilot
  Or a pirate " whisper
  The many stars that answer / to /
  Many
Names.

For what still is

Shuttered in
Watching cardinal red wooden wings
Spinning
   Speak nostalgias of wind
& long gauze skirts
& blue grass festivals
 We leapt & tromped
   To that red fiddle.
The fiddler hands magnificent
Told tendrils
Roots noosing roots cut
   Just in time
For catching the breath
Of some kind of
Lower case god
   In our rough yet
Very naive hands.

A Finch

This is no dress rehearsal/this is
Our life. (The Tragically Hip)

& if I could save the finch now -

I would. Weird, not knowing, not being able to
Find out.   Go back
   Lift its last squeak in my hand
Blow on it once
See if heat of human breath
   Would be of consequence.

With all the redefinitions
Of what "murder " is - these days —
   Maybe we killed it, its bamboo cage
Hanging over the plant stand
Robust with pink-budded cactus
   As, following theatre
Rehearsal the night before, we fed the finch
Iceberg leaves & watered

Its small white bowl.
   The sweet smoke coiled & coupled
As it rose around the bird cage.
We were all kids , good kids bad kids,
   Depending on who asked or was
Asked. If I knew now
That I'd never get blamed or caught
   I'd have dragged myself
   Stoned myself
Flaunted my innocuous guilt in the village

Square. It wasn't a dress rehearsal.
The finch was found dead
   X started laughing
   Y wrecked the car
We had no way to get to
The play we inhabited. Exit off cue

Enter / re-enter off cue
As situation asked

Heart thudding the ocean song
In the conch of our ears. Bird cages are
　　Vows of silence
　　The hurt-hold intimate,
Meant to be broken. Dismantled.
Little pictographic marks left
　　By the prisoner.

　　But some stay, clutch & shroud
The silence —
　　Chosen —
That would make others crazed.

Considering Origami

I talk origami often. Some man
Asked if I really know
  Origami, a good friend. I said
No but I love that word
& promptly

He left me, disillusioned maybe.
I remember being shocked
  At how quick quick
You can be wadded into a ball of
  Headlines
& drowning, skipped like a child

- Stone across the razor-wake river.
Quick quick
  Blood & sweat & spit
Pacts, wash & diffuse like rainbows
Dropped into eyes
  Thud, bone dark within the eye.

Marrow.

The other side of paper

(For J)

Stepping out   from
Myself
   As a dancer might
Step through a slice of paper
Into another edge
   Of stage set

Exit lower left

— I don't want to be a mirror
Of myself.
   As you sleep
I trace the skin of your face
Like the nurse
   Saying "lo what is

The evidence of time"
You stir, I tongue the temple
   Vein or artery & what
Is a temple? Walls
Huff & puff & it's a rough place honey
   Seated on a kitchen chair

Within the accordion folds
Of long term silences
   & secrets
Too large for a single human being
Much too much for
   A book & tree chasing boy.

Blue; the virtues of solitude

(*re* Matisse)

The stage is blue
Matisse paper cut-outs emerge
   Trace the tree ring lines
   Dancing a circle.
It's cool when dancers
   Loosen their fists as they dance
   Touch hands a moment
   Engaging—

Some break off,
Tear the careful cautious
   Dance &
   Entering winds'
   Shuffling death cards
Dance alone
   Into a solitude
   Fists raised to rainforest canopy
   Rage become

Sleep of the unnamed
A separate eco galaxy
   & even the monkeys clatter
   In favor of
The vulnerable shining,
The underdog.

The animation festival - Baltimore 1988

It's a box
  At the animation festival —
A line shifts
Then shifts again
Seems to
Lock
  Then breaks
Over & over
  Stubborn & frail
Like the psyche. I've felt it — guessing
  You have as well.

What is its talisman? That box-echo?
  A drop of water
A jewel,
  A book called The Living Stone
Found in the drawer of the dead?
  Praise quivers
  Posthumous

Like the love of the displaced
  Wild
  Things of all wildernesses —: scavenger
Bear & fox
Even the heart where
You too love deer — flip of
The white tail like giving demons
  The finger. "Screw off"

As they say
  Young buggers
  Who believe they've
  figured out the boxes
& trapdoors
  Of all worlds —:

Cesare's "the Other"

Want to be
more than objectified

A fleck of foam
On a water glass carried to death
More

A cellophane wing
Judged by the wind a wing
Torn from a racehorse fly
Observed
You shift shoes
Jotting notes in a ledger
The master of mutability
& truth's indifference

Blue ash heaped in lit bowl
A thimble
To test dressmaker needle's wit
Scalper of cell & doll & compost
Surgeon of bone & bled out
Soul.

Nuance

The jukebox
    Painted
Black & red, rang out Proud Mary.
Some guy in the back
    Called her
"Girl"

Said "I'm your one true
    Love"

& bashed his beautiful face
In the glass leaded frames
    Cut to a thousand
Prints
From Jamaica. "I am bad cause
I talked back
Why am I bad cause I talked back
I know I'm Mary Mary Mary
Ship of freight
& passenger
The jukeboxes spinning Turn turn turn
As the gasoline & rocks
Shriek down."

Sunbathing

Seating
In a dazed sunshine
That specific burn
Tucked behind clouds

A haze
Deceptive

It was December
It was an island
   Where ferries cut
Through oil spills

(They said
To care for
You take care of you
      & I did oblige
Sometimes— wilful -
The foliage
Rooting
  Marco
Polo call
Halved
         Within the history
Repeated
Just to make sure I remember).

The jetty
Black from the Gulf
Surf
  Hit the flat
Like onyx

     Broke in an ash
Nearly
Human

        & nearby
The world rushed away

A flute trill
Thickened &
   Rolling.

Mouths

1982

"Don't kiss my mouth"
He said.

He had a beautiful mouth
Like gazelles tangential.

Like that Australian
Who came to dinner bearing carrot pie
    & wine

The upper lip jutted
Mildly

Over the brief- bridged lower.

He disappeared over the windowsill
One day
    Lemonade

Shirt tail wagging a bit

& when he returned
To me

Saying "I'm alone now
Come with me"
       A tambourine
    Somewhere in the hills flared black

Jangled
Countered the sky.

    "Kiss
   kiss my
Mouth"
I said. Squirming. Crying.

Him

Old man wandering
Into a bird shop
Asking the clerk for a cockatoo
To replace the dead.
I don't miss him
I've seen that old man in Neil's
Song
Or the window slapped
Open
One Baltimore morning
As the pigeons shit sunrise.

        Ambivalence fierce

    I know
In the 7 circles
He's ok, have that sense
Where he inhabits
The aorta gushing
The entire world
A waterfall.
If that's so
Maybe he's no longer amongst
Those ones
    Unforgiven.

Owning Water

Something about snowmen
& kerosene, got angry
When i said the words back
To them .

    An incredible collision
Those words
When I said the words back
To them

Grooves
    & peaks
Mouthed wholly, mountain
Lozenges. Shuffled gasps,
    No screams.

"

Can someone own a word / words //

"

Water belongs to nobody. X
Keeps saying that, pissed at the claim.
What about the sand, I say
That silk & silt

Getting between my toes.
I laugh a little. We swam naked
In the bay
& neither of us were

Property.

""

Snowmen & kerosene. Maybe
I'm the one who wants
The fences gone

A world that is soluble

At the event of it.
The intent of it.

""

Don't look my husband says
To me: I don't, but ask. It is
      Empathy, not an order.

Sheep lined up along the fence.
I know what he means

Never say goodbye
Before the slaughter

    //. Whale song
      Dolphin Kree
          & sea.

Wandering

Can we be relevant

      Without talking about
The wars & all the wakes & ripple
Effects

Do you want to be a prophet?

     Ha.

Nor a martyr dying for a cause

Past
Gathering clean water for my children
Or grabbing a stone

From someone
About to stone a shadow figment
    Silver
          Lining
In the square.

I like the night

& damn it's been ten days of fever
    Highs
& hell

Finally hatching
I can see the crosswalk

Even though my eyeballs wiggle
& I'm only bubble gum
 Scotch whiskey

In the whimsy

& you can go now

& you can go.

"

The sensor
Winking

Now

Left
Sleeping.

Angels Lie

There's talk
At the
Neighborhood tavern

About riding invertebrate backs of creatures
Across upstate rivers
     & village streams billowing stink

But I hear
    Rainer said it —:
Angels can be terrible beings
     Mating
Monsters — leviathan

Dishonest,
   Wings denuded & useless
In this region raw pink cirrus atmosphere .

  Agents

Glimpsed by toddlers hiding ash & dolls
Under kitchen tables
Picking at their bloodshot piñata
Wartime worn out unicorn
  Eyes.

Driven

(For Bubba)

Going on & on
Trying to feel something
  Ice pick in the rib creased shadow-
Cage, maybe
Letting the owl loose.

Some talk about nothing

  Even that is a weight, nothing,
An anchor my brother dove
To grab but couldn't

Find, almost drowned, fetching
The iron prongs.
   Could've happened to anyone

Tugged from the Susquehanna
Blank & blue
From near- vanishing

   He sat in the boat chair
  Wrapped in a red plaid blanket .
Roused a bit, flushed —

    Daddy offered him
A tin of sardines.

Just going on
& on. Trying to feel.

That book you left unfinished

On the ledge
With some broken shells - pink -

Is something I could have finished
   For you
       Symbiotic as we were

   "

I left it there, open

Growing illegible
In the scented rain.

   "

Sometimes

I take no souvenirs.
   I let the relics sit &
Shiver in the wake

   "

Darling, said the old man on the corner.

The lie never even kissed

Your mouth.

It knew nothing of you.

   "

Don't let it noose you, drag
       Your sunlight downtown
             Where comic books
Lie midst puddles

Blood is thicker, brother.

X

(Elegy for DS)

It's all I have
Wonder how you are, now

On the other side where doves live
    Even though they are strange & dark

In full sight of the cat, slate
Blue as a teapot seated, thudding
Shine of it
      & the hushed dialect of rock

Eroded & grown
In ridge & depth —
     Scattered into
The valley of neon butterflies
Urban/ sea

(Balls of demolition swinging
Errant
    Disco balls spinning)

It's all I have left — wonder.

First teaching

Do they teach
Kids
About the bones
Every bone
Has its story
Whistling
   Whispering

This is what silence is.

Inhabiting Heather

What is chosen
But everyone -: I can sense thirst
    Dehydration

That gut-twist
    Detail of grief
        As of starvation.
      I met a girl once
She seemed inhabited
Her eyes so transparent
    I could see to the back of her skull,
Some nerves, twitching
As she torched
Any living thing on the porch.
        What is chosen, I told her
Is everything—:
Each raw inhale,
    Each rattling of the snake tail.

Civil war is Messy

No need to fight. Civil war
Is messy.   Laying flowers on the boundary

    I kneel in the mud bank.
Summon spider & pig & bull calf
From the eventual
        Into the smudged blueprint
        Lifeline of my wrist, tic tic.
    Shadow
Is useful. Is as it is. Chosen.

The blue flamethrower
  Of sadism
Outed.

Everyone is worthwhile.

It's just another poem.

      & I'd write it on air
If I had to
      Write it
With
Air.

Tribute

Dear Mr x

  Good to hear you're writing again
Those floating haikus
So light
   So substantial
A messenger pigeon could not bear them.

I miss our coffees. I miss knowing
Knowledge so lucent
    & without alphabet —: how you had no fear
Of your mind.

We did not desire each other yet fed
    Laughing
As Allies feed

Upon same rations of salted meat
Of smoked herrings
In baguette.

We were in love with other people
& so cognizant of that boundary
     Doubt did not occur
To us.

If they had trusted us
As we trusted ourselves.

I didn't know you wrote haikus

Crisscross plum tree branches
Shadow gleaning shape
   & form

I know that you love your lady
& coax a cat called Layla
To your lap
As you read & write as the living pages
  Slough cells like skin.

Best to you

C

Gemini X

The time I died
I looked over my shoulder
Each moth pissed-on, each Nazi
    Pissing
        Making me want departure

But some thing pulled back —:
Here // a who a what a place
      A marina
A treehouse a poem interlocking
       arcs, dominion
Of oriental cranes.

The laws of marrying a cryptozoologist

I can see over my shoulder
Bigfoot in blue headlights
  & I know I've known him
    Intimately.

That monster absence
That monster abandon
    That leaving
      Without a goodbye.
"

I hear the barn owl is
Guardian owl & when you tie yourself
    To a tree it's difficult
      Setting yourself afire.

You have to rely on another
To scatter your bones
    To filter your ashes
      From the dome

Of skull. I see over threshold.
"

I don't believe// I believe, immensely
    Play hooky

      figure it out.
Watching from the alley
As my one greatest ally
    Vanishes — damn
      Mistrust , bastard, lurks
Looms a boat
Of its own.

Reading Poe

A house with ache / division / want
A mouth half-kissed
    Aged 16

She saw the Eureka with her body
A shine glimmered behind / within
    The slight traces of

Her ribs
& having hid truant in the brush
    Where pheasant was flushed
    By playing dogs

Having smoked with squirrel & possum

She read Poe aloud
  Now straddling a tree

    She drew close
To the elemental
& believed spirit to be fact

Infusing her bones
Without ridicule //.   Eureka meant
One. Spirit of spirit
    Soul without walls.

Walking Charlie

I guess whispering of snooze buttons
I guess walking the pup come morning
I guess
     Bothering these fissured side streets
     & cracked parking lots

Invoke a limited world erupting
Gleaning the shine of things. Above alL
     This fabulous mutt

Walks a relaxed blue lead
& when he tugs I say "walk
Walk"
     & he does, easy. What else
     Is better than this

But coming home
To your sleeping off a difficult day —:
& me, knowing the secret Braille.

This is my love: This is my stranger

I don't know why we don't pack
Our souls in red vinyl
Suitcases, optimists draped in
Salvation Army boas, black combat
Boots.
      I guess we aren't yet
Ready to float away, cirrus
Orange
Moonlight; ready,
    Leaping the Hudson.

Driving along the Catskills

Snow-creased mountains
Crowded out a pale
    Milky Way
    A red hawk
Dipped & died, quick, force of
The old yellow Chevy fender. Already
    Stricken, you

        Bent
To the hawk, sought wound to
    Mend, perhaps
Some blood, sticky
            To wash
With that old yellow grease rag
    Grabbed from the trunk —:

        I looked away —:
There was no way
        To argue
            The fact of endings:
Your ardor so huge.

Eve candlelight

- 12/24/23, 3.36 pm

> *Every child is a wonder*
> (P.D. Lyons)

— Somewhere
In my brain
The animated drummer strikes

Rhythmically & his lamb just-struck
Levitates

Then falls back into the stitch
Of the breathing.

Never thought a sheep
Was deity-kin,

The wormhole to God opens just an instant —
Outer
& inner space — brevity.

Wick touched tip
To wick
In a circle, soft
With others
Of torn natures, as
An ellipsis, rooting a fire-tree
The traced line of secular palm.

Never read a Hail Mary aloud

(For Delores)

Or silently.
Sat at this round kitchen table; oak
Maybe maple.

Authentic pre-fab grain.

Thin memory garnered tree rings
At center. Visions / worldviews
These glossed paper booklets.

Drawings
Jesus midst awkwardly rehearsed
Genuflections.

I remember our
Father; "who art in heaven," see
Her winces soothed
As we read aloud.

How
Many Hails, floating - when she's the
    One quartered & drawn
Levitating
    Striations, struggler red dawn.

The perspective of telephone wires

Da Vinci said: the ugly too is beautiful
& the boy peered around corners
Pretended he was himself the saxophone
Inhabiting the Mitchell tune
Blue light & bar napkins
Half-sketches & whole-truths
The night he fell in love. There was
Nave. Enclave. There was
Peace amidst the kilned soul of
Spilling bone/ blood/rubble.

He saw a festival card
With dogs & a yellow bird.
I like dogs & birds he said
& the house was painted yellow.
He tucked the image folded
Into his T pocket
Ash rising & sudden
Everything smelled like flowers.

Verdicts

As the drawbridge
Halved   we looked, the expanse of
Sandbar & island
  Fear of heights notwithstanding —:

  We stood
        Our pulse lilting the fall
Amidst roiling foghorn sounds.

      Surely, life seemed
At pause
        Pressure like pelvic arc
          To pelvis
& death distanced.

          A ship passed pea green
Another ship passed scarlet A
  I thought of mouths & thigh & jetty
& truly an instant of ecstasy
So empathetic

      Gentle
          & worries
Tumbled
As mind is a structure's rhapsody —

Succored

The licorice
Lozenge on the curled tongue
Dissolute
As clouds
Sweet.

Mist tendril wove around
Human
Witnessing I knew

The common sensibilities
Of what
We grope to share
& hope lasts — metamorphosis
Transcendence
Change —
Even
As fossil marrow breathes of bone.

Dangling Shoes Going to Brooklyn

All she can see are the shoes
Dangling or crossed
   Tiptoe to toe.
All she can see is the
Looking away
   From faces, especially the eyes
      & as her gaze floats & settles
        Randomly,
Even the smirk & grin seem grim.

 //   Next car down
  Maybe children
Chanting chant chant //

Some young woman's face comes
   Into focus as peripherally red
Platform sneakers & bare ankles in winter
 Swing
    Swinging
& the older woman looks away,
Riddle & epiphany.

Each beautiful face
   Gasping, abandoned,
Youth, vulnerable
& invincible
     The young woman grimaces

Pops some blue chewing gum & like
A child underwater
   Blows
Air, an exhale, one two three, a chorus
Noted

Each passenger the inhale
     An exhale —:

What is manna
But going from Manhattan to Brooklyn

        Through catacombs
Going
  To a realm
        Of flashing visuals
Vendors, cash
Only, a carnival, apathy only a mild
        Charade.

Weight of Squirrels in Winter

(For Alice)

The apartment window frame
Peeling lead dust & neurology
 Shifted.
A bird feeder swung
Like a bare lightbulb
   On a scout-knot string.
Its blue, powder,
Scratching
At bare twigs,
The weight of a fat squirrel.

The lady's dozing.

A photograph of Sinatra
Taped to a broken
Television screen —:
Sucking a cigarette butt
Looking sidelong
Where the camera was uninvited —:
"Did you really write a letter
To
Mussolini
     Or was it just a post it
   Memo
Stuck to the refrigerator."

I don't ask. Sociology claims
The liar's eyes shift & slide
Up & to the peripheral left
That's how I know.
     Honesty. Corrupted
        History.

That's how we know.

Vectors

(For Sinead)

I can read your vibes / figure out
  The bareback runaway horses of
Your mind. The shifting & constancy.

The afternoon rum, it's waiting.

   Haven't tasted rum since I was a kid
Lost on a county bus, riding stop to
Stop, transfers missed, to evade

  That last descent. Someone
Said to me, a gentle infusion — hell
Is here on earth, we make our own —:

   Standing tall before gentle knolls
Distanced Pennsylvania mountains
As a kid in pigtails I thought
           I knew.

When God is relevant

(For Kim Phuc)

Today a man spoke
  As if he was a river spoke
Aloud.   " A photograph
A young girl running
      Ran, her nakedness
Afire. That's what napalm does."
He said.

I can't
Figure out anybody or their horses
      But I'm told: that girl, who has
A name — Kim Phuc— was 9,
Saigon & skyline, rib & marrow —:
Is not a billboard
      Now, or ever. But she was
      An
Image
      Hatched the mirage, brought
        Vietnam to a human door.

Letting go

Raw & violet
As flowers jagged on her sill
His face, hands, from holding
The rope tight, taut, even as he
Desired —: let it go.

""

"Speak," she'd say as to a trained
Clown bicycling in a circle
Or a hound high 5 for a potato chip.

He let go.

""

There was no pain in pain.
Infants too were soldiers.
A refugee spoke of gratitude
& amidst flash & battery,
He heard he was amazed.

""

The monkeys
Swung in the canopy, clattered.
It was a flash, another place.
He was a flash, himself
A lightning struck zing

& all around the core
Of love the chants, the singing.

Note to self

What made you
Lean your head back
    & feel your sawed open flank
Dissolve
Into the blank

& forgive the nature
Of bone// the nature of blank.
    Gasp, fire eaters.

"

        What made you
Stop trusting the steady
Force of mountains mist-swathed
 Swathed
     Like a precious
Orangutan

On the precipice

"

       What made you turn your face
 Look over your shoulder sudden
& know the resilience
      Mystery strange & reeking sulphuric

   Of what is sure, of

What you guess
    At this
       Instant
         is sure.

Can't own an iguana

(For CW my friend)

Catherine took care of
        An iguana.
          Colors beige or khaki or kaleidoscopic
    A professor by the sea
She weeping read Finnegan as I talked to
        What the iguana feasted upon
            Lettuce & the memory

Of allies midst buds of pink cacti.
    Allies. Hands sticky as friends break
Thick wedged
Honeycomb & froth
    Of good dark beer & tavern laughter.

            We get lost or

People go // we are no hotel,
    Silver diners, cresting the urban edge.
        There are no guessed & mesmerizing
Numbers pinned over each door
        Each entry, foyer, red exit.

It's random, this sense //
Kinship.
            Anyone who's walked the tracks
Midst dust clouding
        The bloodshot
                Eyes

Nearly exhausted from too
Much wonder.

Night of Parkland School Shooting

A drawing of a photograph

He drew the night
Of yet another shooting — a sketch.
    Kids
  A woman a man
     Perhaps a few younger children

Straddling thin blue bicycles with
Great blue wheels
  & trees rattling like ribs
    Along the Hudson
& water like goose shivers
Throwing the light back
In little sunlit spears

Amnesia

Once a boy slung her over his
Shoulder
— Not her, but a thing resembling —
    & she was the weight
Shadow takes

When left
        On the low sandbar
    Midwinter
If all the ferries were asleep
As fish under ice

A red flash a flare.
Catch catch me catch me
    She said
It's an ephemeral pact // both
    A truth & a dare.

Untitled

(For Irene)

I like that poem about a tree.
She was that poem
    About a tree. Irreverence
Thin & scarcely clad like bells —

  A said "her childhoods
Sound like part Disney & part midnight
Crypt."   I too saw dark glitter.
The seagulls, wind catching their
Backs.
   One night she talked me
Into believing there was no soul.
I let void settle in my ribcage
For a moment, an hour. It was easier

To believe the emptiness.
Yet the emptiness too was alive
  Tendrils of fog
Spiraling in & out of the body,
   Warm as noon in summer.

The Dog Who Loved Sweet Potato pie

(For Ben)

    Black bay of hounds near
The river-bend, grey bedrock

Headlines
Newsprint confetti piled along
A pile red socks & sweaters
    The bored dog chewed.

Pink

      A pile of pink peaches
& Louisiana hot sauce herring in tins /
    Houseboat / bomb shelter.

Yellow scotch frothing deckhand
    Men once-shadows —?—.

Unforgettable & forgiven such ghosts
Build
From splint & scratch
An old hospital threadbare, spun
Foundation
           Angel-spit
Borne like a wet sac of baby
Spiders
      On farm-fact breeze.

Keep scrawling love

"I love love love"

An epitaph that makes demigods

Laugh & shred

The sun's coronal flare

   Someone is talking
      Someone is

Hearing the desert cacti & molted scales
Rattling as pens skin boulder,
Paper & newspaper skin of shaman

Who do the dirty

Work some gods call in.

Tracing a leaf

Damn I say; you remember every
Detail/ find resonance of a greater history
In every filigree leaf.

      In one coral reef fragment floating
    Mirror on mirror—:
Mirroring not you
But the Gemini dark of others .   (The

  Shine built around a graveyard)
Most of all
Maybe

      You can discern —
The meaning of my
Own fingerprints,   better than a twin,   you

Could tell / hear the sea
   Within the shell.

scarecrows fly // Dear Children, Aware

// Dear my youth

    kicked out of cinemas
For tugging the end of a cigarette
As the woman on screen cupped
Her hand over the dead cigarette
As the lit match neared
& the world leaned in.

    Kicked out of libraries
For laughing too
Loudly
Love
"Really as I
Drive into the cougar's
Jaws I am not blaming you" creeks

& riverbeds course through

Black n white TVs

Once roaches fell from the ceiling like plums
    Upon my eyes
As we read Brecht & clouds of plum tree
Feathers
    A peeping Tom whispered

" Youth is
Fascist"

    Pale head on the cedar
    & dead horseflies torn from their wings
Of vinyl pressed to cellophane

Sage of peace

Big green eyes.

Always trying to explain

Small hands fluttering
    Peach-fuzz eyelashes in a breeze subzero
  "Go out upon the world "
& it was a way of being
    More
Than quest, less than
Sustainable —

Explaining

The soul's membrane bounced each
    Word back, echo
Split like birdcall
    Red rubber ball kicked, wall on wall
The knee of blue jeans
    Tears flesh, she
Lifts her arms in a rapt
    Sunlike salutation
"Go , with joy" —

It wasn't impossible, really.
It didn't matter
    If it mattered. Her heart ticked
The click of a walking stick
Braided asp & bone.
& the water burned
    Sun scratching snow.

Glimpsed
The flash / the tree of living
Brindle swans

(For Doctors Without Borders.)

We are not cloth rag dolls
Pulled from mosaics, sheer tissue
Paper, tissue
   To shed to shear to sketch
Upon.

We are not plastic sex robots
Creatures of dime store manikins
Empty in the shopfront
    Eyes fixed on axis
Like dead blue stars. Indeed
  Are we

      Human beings afloat
Red
     Cellos
  So impossible that they could
 Halt
War —

     —

It's dehumanizing, what calls it out,
This inner wall (" how many walls
Can one man build" he said
   Cause I freaked out
Just cause he said the word of truth
  Sinatra never sings.

& in the trench doctors lay bodies
As if they are planting -
Faces kind, must be something
   Better —/ a tool rattling in air caught
Between, in serrated

71

Bloody edges, closing around a swan.

    Sweetheart
In the instant of knowing
What is it you see.

Planetarium Specks

"What is your sadness" she asked

"What is your joy" he asked

    Speck
        Stuck
Black on screen flat
Between them
Speck
    Stirred.
The dogs /
The humans /
Paka white rat
     Epiphanies / each

Caught their breath raptly /

     Bright flashing lizard tongues —
Catching the indeterminate
   Summons
Gazing close
   Addiction beneath a tree.

Shimmering broken bicycles //
Pedaling
   Cats & clowns who
Forgot their training—

     ("Are you a gnat or a butterfly")
("Catching
Someone else's exhale
Is the greatest dare.") ("The instinctive
Call
Of such things is fragile &
     Random,
     As should be.")

Laying Flowers on the Boundary

He used to throw it
My way. "Transgressions of
Boundary are what is
Key

   Darling" —:

 One Friday night
Sharing a bottle of scotch
Suckling the
Bitter lemon twists

We necked mildly

That's all. Shimmering profiled black
  Cat-in-the-window
Streetlamp

& our transgression completed
Itself
    The moon brightened
  Orgasmed
& dropped behind brownstone
Roofs

Where shadow puppetry played
  Purple & gray

& in dream alone, perhaps
  We lay lilies &
Wrist-corsages prom & peace
    Where dance & trench
    The boundary
     Creased our world.

www.ingramcontent.com/pod-product-compliance
Lightning Source LLC
Chambersburg PA
CBHW030726180526
45157CB00008BA/3062